French vocabulary for GCSE

In topic categories, with memory techniques and tips

Table of contents

Introduction

Not all students are good at retaining vocabulary. Differences in short and long-term memory skills, together with differing approaches to the stress of learning all go towards making a very uneven playing field when it comes to performance in exams.

I wrote this book to help students remember words without having to spend hours learning lists by heart. As well as setting out the material by topic, I have focussed on sharing my memory techniques. There's no point in knowing the word for cinema if you can't say you went there, no point in knowing how to say chips if you can't say you ate them. French is notorious for its articles and prepositions, and what students need is the confidence to use them. My quirky methods will help you conquer these tricky areas. You may of course choose not to use them, you may not need them, and you may have your own, which is all great – whatever works for you!

Equally, with the question of the gender of nouns, there are no hard and fast rules for knowing and remembering whether a word takes "un" or "une" but with the help of my visual techniques, students soon master what used to be a minefield to them.

These methods have been tried, tested and developed over ten years of teaching and I relish every instance where I have watched the lightbulb go on when a student suddenly realises how easy it is to remember something they had no understanding of before.

This book is intended to accompany my previous book in the series "How to Ace your French Oral" and used together these two handbooks will without doubt improve any student's performance in French. In particular, this book will help students enrich and vary their own oral and written answers, allowing them to adapt my answers to suit them.

Please note that this is intended to be a study aid rather than a comprehensive guide to the entirety of the French language, and my "rules" may have exceptions in places but I have taken care not to claim otherwise!

I wish you all success with your language studies and welcome any feedback you may have via my website www.lucymartintuition.co.uk

Bonne chance!

Vocabulary for reading and listening

In the reading and listening papers, there will be a good deal of vocabulary that you know, not through active learning, but through your own common sense. As we share lots of common Latin roots, there are dozens, maybe even hundreds of cognates in French. Here are just a few of them – you will notice rules emerging such as words ending in -ity in English will end in -ité in French, and words ending in -ation are usually identical in both languages:

Some common cognates

absence (absence)

ballet (ballet)

danse (dance

calculatrice (calculator)

débat (debate)

édition (edition)

festival (festival)

horreur (horror)

impression (impression)

juin (june)

kilometre (kilometer)

liberté (liberty)

musique (music)

nombre (number)

opéra (opera)

peintre (painter)

raison (reason)

statut (status)

transaction (transaction)

univers (universe)

wagon (wagon)

xylophone (xylophone)

yaourt (yogurt)

zéro (zero)

absolu (absolute)

britannique (british)

catholique (catholic)

dramatique (dramatic)

entier (entire)

fréquent (frequent)

graduel (gradual)

horrible (horrible)

illégal (illegal)

logique (logical)

mental (mental)

nerveux (nervous)

ordinaire (ordinary)

romantique (romantic)

sincère (sincere)

traditionnel (traditional)

urgent (urgent)

vulnérable (vulnerable)

abandonner (abandon)

bloquer (block)

capturer (capture)

détruire (destroy)

établir (establish)

finir (finish)

gouverner (govern)

identifier (identify)

limiter (limit)

mentionner (mention)

footballeur (footballer)

rappeur (rappeur)

directeur (director)

ingénieur (engineer)

visiteur (visitor)

noter (note)

observer (observe)

posséder (possess)

qualifier (qualify)

poster (post – online)

internet (internet)

tchatter (chat – online)

week-end (weekend)

influencer (influence)

recycler (recycle)

répondre (respond)

étudier (study)

transformer (transform)

unir (unite)

varier (vary)

université (university)

qualité (quality)

quantité (quantity)

société (society)

diversité (diversity)

productivité (productivity)

acceptabilité (acceptability)

reservation (reservation)

conversation (conersation)

génération (generation)

nation (nation)

population (population)

intégration (integration)

exploitation (exploitation)

concentration (concentration)

RELATIONSHIPS AND DESCRIBING PEOPLE

Family

dans ma famille	in my family
nous sommes quatre	there are 4 of us
mon père	my father
ma mère	my mother
mes parents	my parents
ainé / cadet	older / younger (m)
ainée / cadette	older / younger (f)
mes grands parents	my grandparents
mon cousin / ma cousine	my cousin
mon oncle	my uncle
ma tante	my aunt
Je suis enfant unique	I'm an only child
le bébé	baby
le mari	husband
la femme	wife / woman
le garçon	boy
Mon frère s'appelle	my brother is called
Je n'ai **pas de** sœur	I don't have a sister

Top tip: How to use s'appelle and qui s'appelle

s'appelle = is called, **qui s'appelle** = who is called

J'ai un frère qui s'appelle Charlie= I have a brother called

Mon frère s'appelle Charlie = my brother is called Charlie

How you get on – *use "on"!*

on s'entend bien	*we get on well*
beaucoup en commun	*lots in common*
on aime	we like
les mêmes choses	*the same things*
on se dispute	*we argue*
la même musique	*the same music*

Adjectives to describe people

Je suis	I am
Il / elle est	he / she is
grand(e)	tall
petit(e)	small
gros(se)	fat
mince	thin
intéressant(e)	interesting
ennuyeux/-euse	boring
sympa	nice
embêtant(e)	annoying
vieux (vieille)	old
jeune	young
sportif/-ive	sporty
paresseux/-euse	lazy
gentil (gentille)	kind
égoïste	selfish
beau (belle)	beautiful

joli(e)	pretty
laid(e)	ugly
fort(e)	strong
faible	weak
méchant(e)	naughty
agréable	pleasant
désagréable	unpleasant
bavard(e)	chatty
silencieux /-ieuse	silent
marrant(e)	funny
sérieux/-euse	serious
poli(e)	polite
impoli(e)	impolite
triste	sad
fâché(e)	angry
heureux/-euse	happy
sensible	sensitive
de bonne humeur	in a good mood
de mauvaise humeur	in a bad mood
fatigué	tired
énergique	energetic
prudent(e)	careful
maladroit(e)	clumsy
facile à vivre	easygoing
difficile	fussy

Hair adjectives

longs / courts	long / short
raides	straight
frisés / bouclés	curly
blonds / roux / marron	blonde / red / brown
J'ai les cheveux raides	I have straight hair
Il a les cheveux marron *(no s!)*	he has brown hair
Il est chauve	he is bald

General appearance

Il porte des lunettes	he wears glasses
une barbe	beard
une moustache	moustache
Je ressemble à	I look like
On se ressemble	we look similar

General adjectives

plein(e) / vide	full
sain(e)	healthy
malsain	unhealthy
facile	easy
difficile	difficult
chaud(e)	hot
froid(e)	cold
moderne	modern
ancien (-ienne)	old

individuel(le)	detached
jumelé(e)	semi-detached
cher	expensive
bon marché	cheap
payant	paying (not free)
gratuit	free
sec (sèche)	dry
mouillé(e)	wet
léger (légère)	light
lourd(e)	heavy
lent(e)	slow
rapide	fast
génial(e)	great
pénible	awful
sale	dirty
propre	clean
nouveau (nouvelle)	new
étroit(e)	narrow
large	wide

Half / step- and in-laws

This is where it gets complicated – demi can be step or half, and beau / belle can be step or in law – so best avoided!

mon demi-frère	my stepbrother or half brother
ma demi-sœur	my stepsister or half sister
ma belle-mère	my stepmother or mother-in-law
mon beau-père	my stepfather or father-in-law

mon beau-frère   my brother-in-law

ma belle-sœur   my sister-in-law

Types of relationship and family

toutes sortes de familles	all sorts of families
de bons rapports	good relations
une relation	a relationship
draguer	to chat up
petit copain	boyfriend
petite copine	girlfriend
un rendez-vous	a date
sortir avec	to go out with
tomber amoureux	to fall in love
l'amour	love
rencontrer	to meet
épouser	to marry
un couple	a couple
fidèle	faithful
ensemble	together (musical)
cohabiter	to live together
avant de se marier	before getting married
se marier avec	to marry
divorcé	divorced
marié	married
séparé	separated
une famille nombreuse	a big family
des familles recomposées	blended families
familles monoparentales	single parent families

le mariage gay	gay marriage
se disputer	to argue
plaquer	to dump (someone)
la valeur	value
la stabilité	stability
élever un enfant	to bring up a child
adopter	to adopt
les parents adoptifs	adoptive parents
la famille d'acceuil	adoptive family

HOME – (chez moi)

> **Top tip: Mum owns the house, car, road, the whole town...**
>
> *Notice that all the rooms in the house, and a lot of the things around the house are **feminine** (house, door, window, car, shelves, wardrobe, TV). Imagine that the only place Dad is allowed is office and sitting room – and garden. He can also have a bed, a computer, a pen and a few other bits (see second list below) but he has to do the housework (le ménage).*

une maison individuelle	a detached house
une maison jumelé	a semi-detached house
une maison mitoyenne	a terraced house
une cuisine	a kitchen
une salle à manger	a dining room
une salle de bains	a bathroom
une chambre	a bedroom
une véranda	a conservatory

une voiture	a car
une table	a table
une armoire *(keep your armour there)*	a wardrobe
une étagère *(has étages like floors)*	a bookshelf
une chaise	a chair
une porte	a door
une fenêtre	a window
une lampe	a lamp
une commode	a chest of drawers
une piscine	a swimming pool
une machine à laver	a washing machine
une cuisinière	a cooker
une télévision	a TV
une Xbox / Playstation	Xbox / Playstation
une ville	a town
une rue	a road

Picture Dad in these rooms only

un salon	a sitting room
un jardin	a garden
un grenier	an attic
un bureau	an office

He can sit on

un canapé	a sofa
un fauteuil	an armchair

un lit — a bed

For entertainment he can have

un livre — a book

un ordinateur — a computer

un crayon — a pencil

un stylo — a pen

un lave-vaisselle — a dishwasher

Top tip: Describing where things are in the house

*Imagine you're walking round a new house, you keep discovering new floors "Oh! First floor!" "Oh! Second floor!") In French this is "**au** premier étage" and "**au** deuxième étage"*

Daily routine

Je me réveille — I wake up

Je me lève — I get up

Je me douche — I shower

Je me brosse les dents — I brush my teeth

Je m'habille — I get dressed

Je descends — I go downstairs

Je prends mon petit déjeuner — I have my breakfast

Je vais au collège — I go to school

Je rentre chez moi — I go home

Je fais mes devoirs — I do my homework

en regardant la télé — while watching TV

Weekend routine differences

Je fais la grasse matinée	I have a lie-in
Je sors avec mes amis	I go out with my friends
Je me détends	I relax
Je ne fais rien	I do nothing
Je passe la journée au lit	I spend the day in bed
Je le mérite!	I deserve it!

Jobs around the house

pour gagner	in order to earn
mon argent de poche	my pocket money
Je passe l'aspirateur	I vacuum
Je fais la vaisselle	I wash up *(think: vessels)*
Je lave la voiture	I wash the car *(think : lather)*
Je range ma chambre	I tidy my room
Je prépare le diner	I make dinner
Je mets la table	I lay the table *(think : meh)*
Je débarrasse la table	I clear the table
Je sors les poubelles	I take the rubbish out

Not helping at home

Je ne fais rien	I don't do anything
Je n'ai pas le temps	I don't have time
Ils nous donnent	they give us
trop de devoirs	too much homework
plus important	more important

mon brevet	GCSE equivalent
Je suis en train de	I'm in the middle of

Example

Il faut que je fasse des tâches ménagères afin de gagner mon argent de poche, et je pense que c'est important d'aider avec le ménage, mais les profs nous donnent trop de devoirs et en ce moment je suis en train de préparer mon brevet, donc je ne fais pas beaucoup.

I have to do household chores to earn my pocket money and I think it's important to help with housework but the teachers give us too much homework, and at the moment I'm in the middle of revising for my GCSEs, so I don't do much.

TOWN AND TRANSPORT (la ville, les transports)

Describing your town

ce que j'aime	what I like
c'est qu'il y a	is that there is
tout ce dont j'ai besoin	everything I need
où on peut	where one can
Je vais **au**	I go to the *(masc nouns)*
Je suis allé **au**	I went to the *(masc nouns)*
Je vais **à la**	I go to the *(fem nouns)*
Je suis allé **à la**	I went to the *(fem nouns)*

Masculine places in the town – take "au"

le cinéma (je vais au cinéma)	cinema
le restaurant	restaurant

le collège	school
le parc	park
le café	cafe
le centre commercial	shopping centre
le centre sportif	sports centre
le coiffeur	hairdresser *(quiff)*
le supermarché	supermarket

> *Feminine places in town – think holiday :* go to the bank for money, the library for books, the station to get the train, to the pool, beach, ice rink, then the post office

la banque (je vais à la banque)	bank
la bibliothèque	library
la gare	station
la piscine	pool
la plage	beach
la patinoire	ice rink
la poste	post office

> If they begin with a vowel, use **à l'**
>
> Je vais / je suis allé **à l'**école / église / hypermarché
>
> *I go / I went to school, to church, to the hypermarket*

Transport

*All transport that has an **en**gine uses "en"*

en voiture	by car
en avion	by plane
en bus	by bus
en bateau	by boat
en car	by coach
à pied / à vélo	on foot / by bike

On foot and bike, your legs hurt – ah!

Directions

tout droit	straight on
à droite	right
à gauche	left
aux feux	at the traffic lights
au carrefour	at the crossroads

Shopping

l'argent de poche	pocket money
économiser	to save
dépenser	to spend
gaspiller	to waste
un portefeuille	wallet
les soldes	the sales
faire du lèche vitrine	to go window shopping

Trains

le guichet	ticket office
un billet simple	a single ticket
un billet aller-retour	a return ticket

c'est quel quai?	Which platform is it?
le consigne de bagages	left luggage

Road accidents

un pneu crevé	a flat tyre
un accident	an accident
un embouteillage	a traffic jam
en panne	broken down
le moteur	the engine
les urgences	the emergency services
les pompiers	the fire brigade
une ambulance	ambulance
un gendarmes	policeman
un policier	policeman
heurter	to hit, crash into *(hurt!)*
le frein	brake
freiner	to brake
faire le plein	fill up with petrol
l'essence	petrol
la ceinture de sécurité	seat belt
la vitesse	speed
un amende	a fine
un témoin	a witness
le témoignage	testimony
blessé	injured
malade	ill
se casser la jambe	to break one's leg
se casser le bras	to break one's arm

EDUCATION AND EMPLOYMENT

School

J'étudie	I study
l'histoire	history
l'informatique	ICT
l'anglais	English
les maths	maths
les sciences	science
le sport	sport
le latin	Latin
le dessin	art
le français	French
la géographie	geography
la musique	music
l'EPS	PE
dans mon collège	in my school
des salles de classe	classrooms
des laboratoires	laboratories
des terrains de sport	sports fields
une bibliothèque	a library
des contrôles	tests
des examens	exams
une cantine	cantine
un théâtre	theatre
un cours	lesson
une cour	playground
ma matière préférée	my favourite subject

neuf cours par jour	9 lessons a day
chaque cours dure	each lesson lasts
pendant la récréation	during break time
la pause déjeuner	lunch break
Je suis fort(e) en	I'm good at
Je suis nul(le) en	I'm bad at
J'ai de bonnes notes	I get good marks
J'ai de mauvaises notes	I get bad marks
J'en ai marre	I'm sick of it
J'en ai ras le bol	I've had enough
les cours devraient	lessons should
commencer plus tard	begin later
Si je pouvais	if I could
je supprimerais les maths	I'd get rid of maths
la règlementation	the rules
strict(e)	strict
on doit	one must
il faut	you have to
on peut	one can
on ne peut pas	one cannot
avoir le droit de	to be allowed to
on n'a pas le droit de	we're not allowed to
porter des bijoux	to wear jewellery
utiliser les portables	to use mobiles
parler en classe	to talk in lessons
sécher les cours	to bunk off lessons
un voyage scolaire	school trip
interne	a boarder

un jour de congé	a day off
préparer le bac	to do A levels
faire une stage en entreprise	do work experience
continuer mes études	to continue studying

> **Top tip:** *Ma matière **préférée** (my favourite subject) – it's your favourite – so 3 cheers and 3 UP (acute) accents*
>
> ***Je préfère** (I prefer) – you prefer it, you're not that sure, the accents look like sad eyebrows (one acute, one grave)*

After leaving school

Je travaille dur	I work hard
pour que je puisse	so that I can
trouver un bon travail	find a good job
le chômage	unemployment
travailler	to work
Il travaille comme	he works as a
un boulot, un métier, un emploi	job
bien payé	well-paid
à plein temps	full-time
à temps partiel	part-time
un travail temporaire	a temporary job
un travail permanent	a permanent job
il faut poser sa candidature	you have to apply
gagner un bon salaire	earn a good salary
beaucoup de chômage	high unemployment
un vendeur / une vendeuse	salesperson
un / une professeur	teacher

un chauffeur	driver
un facteur	postman *(factory of letters)*
un médecin	doctor *(medicine)*
un pharmacien	chemist
un chirurgien	surgeon *(shurgeon)*
un comptable	accountant
un avocat / une avocate	lawyer *(advocate)*
un informaticien /-ienne	IT consultant
un / une secrétaire	secretary
un serveur / une serveuse	waiter
un ingénieur	engineer
un pompier	fireman *(pumps)*
un plombier	plumber *(pb= lead)*
un gendarme	policeman
un infirmier / une infirmière	nurse *(infirmary)*
un coiffeur / -euse	hairdresser *(quiff)*
un photographe	photographer
un commerçant	shopkeeper
un ouvrier / une ouvrière	worker
un homme d'affaires	businessman
une femme au foyer	housewife

Top tip: *if you are talking about what you want to be, there is **no need to say un or une** – so just say "je voudrais être prof"*

LEISURE AND HOLIDAYS (loisirs et vacances)

Playing games

jouer au foot, rugby, cricket	to play football etc
jouer aux échecs	to play chess
jouer aux cartes	to play cards
jouer à l'ordinateur	to play on computer
jouer à la Xbox	to play Xbox

Playing instruments

jouer du piano	to play piano
jouer du violon	to play violin
jouer de la guitare	to play guitar
jouer de la clarinette	to play clarinet
jouer de la batterie	to play drums

Activities - masculine

faire du sport	to do sport
faire du patinage	to go skating
faire du vélo / cyclisme	to go cycling
faire du VTT	mountain biking
faire du shopping	to go shopping
faire du skate	to skateboard
faire du ski	to go skiing
faire du ski-nautique	to go waterskiing
faire du jardinage	to do gardening
faire du bricolage	to do DIY
faire du camping	to go camping

Activities - feminine

faire de la natation	to go swimming
faire de la voile	sailing
faire de la planche à voile	windsurfing *(plank sail)*
faire de la plongée	diving *(plunge)*
faire de la gymnastique	gymnastics
faire de la danse	dance
faire de la musculation	weight training

and if it begins with a vowel "faire de l'"

faire de l'équitation	to go horseriding
faire de l'athlétisme	athletics
faire de l'escrime	fencing *(scream!)*
faire de l'escalade	climbing *(escalator)*
faire de l'alpinisme	mountaineering *(alps)*

and if it's plural "faire des"

faire des promenades	to go for walks
faire des randonnées	to go hiking

Other hobbies

J'aime la lecture	I like reading
lire	to read

aller à la pêche	to go fishing
collectionner	to collect
des timbres	stamps
dessiner	to draw
chanter	to sing
danser	to dance
tricoter	to knit

Cinema and TV

le dernier film que j'ai vu	the last film I saw
il s'agit de	it's about
je l'aime	I like it
je l'ai aimé	I liked it
ça me fait rire	it makes me laugh
passionnant	exciting
mon émission préférée	my favourite show
je le trouve	I find it
un journal	newspaper
les dessins animés	cartoons
les actualités / les infos	the news
quotidien	daily
hebdomadaire	weekly
les feuilletons	soaps
les documentaires	documentaries
la téléréalité	reality TV
les jeux télévisés	game shows
la chaine	channel
l'écran	screen

les téléspectateurs	viewers
les auditeurs	listeners
les vedettes	film stars
la zapette	the remote control
les films romantiques	romantic films
les films d'action	action films
les films d'horreur	horror films
les films de guerre	war films
les films de science-fiction	sci fi films
les films d'aventures	adventure films
les films policiers	detective filims

On holiday– en vacances

je suis allé	I went
j'ai passé	I spent (time)
quinze jours	a fortnight
au bord de la mer	by the sea
au camping	at the campsite
en montagne	in the mountains
en colonie de vacances	on a holiday camp
en ville	in the city
nous avons logé	we stayed
dans un hôtel	in a hotel
dans une auberge	at a hostel
dans un appartement	in an appartment
dans une gite	in a gite
à la station balnéaire	at the holiday resort
à la station de ski	at the ski resort

louer	to hire
nous avons loué	we hired
les valises	suitcases
à l'étranger	abroad
j'ai perdu mon passeport	I lost my passport
retardé	delayed
le vol	the flight
a été annulé	was cancelled
J'ai raté l'avion	I missed the plane
il y avait du monde	it was crowded
avec vue sur	with a view over
avec balcon	with a balcony
faire les valises	to pack suitcases
défaire les valises	to unpack
se bronzer	to sunbathe
se détendre	to relax
se reposer	to rest
se baigner	to swim
se souvenir de	to remember
visiter des monuments	to visit monuments
visiter des musées	to visit the museums
prendre des photos	to take photos
goûter les plats régionaux	to sample local dishes
acheter des cadeaux	to buy presents
se faire des amis	to make friends
les sites touristiques	tourist attractions
Il a fait beau	the weather was good
Il a plu deux fois	it rained twice

une canicule	a heatwave
J'ai envie d'y retourner	I'd like to go back there
J'ai hâte d'y aller	I can't wait to go there
le meilleur pays	the best country
J'ai eu de la chance	I was lucky

NEW TECHNOLOGY (les nouvelles technologies)

mon portable	my mobile
mon ordinateur	my computer
je m'en sers pour	I use it to
envoyer des messages	to send messages
télécharger de la musique	to download music
accéder à l'internet	to go on the internet
rester à la page	to stay up to date
mettre à jour	to update
mon profil Facebook	my Facebook profile
rester en contact	to stay in touch
j'y suis accro	I'm addicted to it
scotché à l'écran	glued to the screen
je ne pourrais pas m'en passer	I couldn't do without it
le cyber-intimidation	cyber-bullying
les inconnus	strangers
le vol d'identité	identity theft
les sites de rencontre	chat rooms
les réseaux sociaux	social networks
rencontrer en ligne	to meet online
une tablette	tablet
un logiciel malveillant	malware

ENVIRONMENT AND SOCIAL PROBLEMS
(l'environnement et les problèmes sociaux)

> **Top tip:** *The three big environment issues **rhyme***
>
> Les gaz d'echappement causent....
>
> | | |
> |---|---|
> | **la pollution de l'air** | air pollution |
> | **le réchauffement de la terre** | global warming |
> | **l'effet de serre** | greenhouse effect |

le changement climatique	climate change
la déeforestation	deforestation
la pluie acide	acid rain
les tremblements de terre	earthquakes
l'énergie nucléaire	nuclear energy
les ressources naturelles	natural resources
en danger	in danger
les espaces verts	green spaces
la circulation	traffic
es embouteillages	traffic jams
les camions	lorries
les usines	factories
la sècheresse	drought
les inondations	floods (innundated)
les incendies	fires
les ordures / déchets	rubbish
la déchetterie	the tip

les poubelles	bins
le déboisement	deforestation

> **Top tip:** Imagine having a shower, then turning the light off, going down and putting out the recycling, getting on the bus and going shopping for green products…

Je me douche	I shower
Je ferme les robinets	I turn the taps off
pour économiser de l'eau	to save water
J'éteins les lumières	I turn off the lights
Je recycle les emballages	I recycle packaging
J'utilise	I use
les transports en commun	public transport
J'achète	I buy
des produits écologiques	green products
on doit / il faut	we must
continuer à	to carry on
J'essaie de	I try to
Je fais des efforts pour	I make an effort to
protéger	to protect
éteindre	to switch off
fermer les robinets	to turn off the taps
économiser	to save
recycler	to recycle
trier	to sort out

les emballages	packaging
le verre	glass
le plastique	plastic
le carton	cardboard
utiliser	to use
acheter	to buy
éviter	to avoid
voyager	to travel
manifester contre	to protest against

Social issues

la pauvreté	poverty
la faim	hunger
le terrorisme	terrorism
l'immigration	immigration
accueillir	to welcome
le racisme	racism
le chômage	unemployment
le taux	the rate
est en hausse	is going up
le manque de	the lack of
l'obésité	obesity
la malbouffe	junk food
les sans-abris	the homeless

les SDF (sans domicile fixe)	the homeless
Il faut qu'on fasse	we must do
quelque chose	something
quelque chose d'utile	something useful
pour les aider	to help them
les défavorisés	the less fortunate
le travail bénévole	voluntary work
les organisations caritatives	charities
les bénévoles	charity workers
consacrer du temps	to devote time
collecter de l'argent	to raise money
sensibiliser	to make aware

WEATHER (le temps)

il fait beau	the weather is good
il fait mauvais	the weather is bad
il fait chaud	it's hot
il fait froid	it's cold

*With things you can see or feel, say **il y a** = there is*

il y a du vent	it's windy
il y a du soleil	it's sunny
il y a des nuages	it's cloudy
il y a du brouillard	it's foggy

il y a de la brume	it's misty

And if things are falling out of the sky, use the verb!

il neige	it's snowing
il grêle	it's hailing
il pleut	it's raining

But watch out for irregularities with pleuvoir

il a plu	it rained
il va pleuvoir	it is going to rain
la pluie	rain

More weather terms

il fait un froid de canard	it's freezing
il pleut à verse	it's pouring
des averses	showers
le ciel est couvert	it is overcast *(covered)*
la météo	weather forecast
la chaleur	heat *(from chaud)*
la canicule	heatwave
le tonnerre	thunder (*a tonne in the air*)
un orage	storm *(rage)*
une tempête	storm
un éclair	flash of lightning

des éclaircies	sunny spells
frappé par la foudre	struck by lightning
une nuit fraiche	a cold night
dans le nord	in the north
dans le sud	in the south
dans l'est	in the east
dans l'ouest	in the west

FOOD, HEALTH AND BODY

Top tip: The food I ate today is un, une, du de la or des

Un / une – if you eat / drink / want the whole thing

Most fruit is feminine, so imagine ladies eating fruit

une poire	pear
une pomme	apple
une banane	banana
une pèche	peach
une orange	orange
une mandarine	satsuma
une mangue	mango
une pastèque	watermelon
une cerise	cherry
une fraise	strawberry
une framboise	raspberry
une prune	plum

Except

un ananas	a pineapple
un melon	a melon
un pamplemousse	a grapefruit
un abricot	an apricot

Steak with salad, followed by tart with ice cream and a cold drink FOR LADIES!

une salade	salad
une entrecôte	a steak
une tarte	a tart
une glace	an ice cream
une boisson	a drink
une limonade	a lemonade
une bière	a beer

Stodgy food, spirits and hot drinks FOR MEN!

un œuf	an egg
un croissant	a croissant
un pain au chocolat/raisin	a pastry
un biscuit	a biscuit
un gâteau	a cake
un sandwich	a sandwich
un chocolat chaud	a hot chocolate
un café	a coffee
un thé	a tea
un whisky	a whisky
(except **un** jus d'orange	an orange juce)

Du - with masculine foods – think PICNIC

du pain	bread
du vin	wine
du boursin	(a type of french cheese)
du beurre	butter (bu- - er)
du fromage	cheese
du poulet	chicken
du jambon	ham
du canard	duck
du saucisson	sausage
du salami	salami
du bœuf	beef
du poisson	fish
du thon	tuna
du pâté	pâté
du gâteau	cake
du chocolat	chocolate
du sel	salt
du miel	honey
du sucre	sugar
du lait	milk

"De la" - feminine foods are on the RED LIST

de la viande	meat *(red meat)*
de la confiture	jam *(strawberry jam)*
de la glace	ice cream *(strawberry)*
de la pizza	pizza *(tomato pizza)*
de la soupe	soup *(tomato soup)*

de la sauce	sauce (tomato sauce)

"De l' if there is some of it and it starts with a vowel

de l'agneau	lamb
de l'eau	water

Plural food – if you eat / have lots, use « des »

des chips	crisps (not chips !!!!)
des frites	chips (fries!)
des escargots	snails
des céréales	cereal (plural cereals)
des pâtes	pasta (plural pastas)
des œufs	eggs
des légumes	vegetables
des pommes de terre	potatoes
des carottes	carrots
des petits pois	peas (little peas)
des haricots verts	green beans
des champignons	mushrooms (champions)
des oignons	onions
des choux de Bruxelles	brussels sprouts
des fruits	fruit
des cerises	cherries
des fraises	strawberries
des framboises	raspberries
des raisins	grapes
des raisins secs	raisins (dry grapes)
des saucisses	sausages

des crêpes	pancakes
des bonbons	sweets
des fruits de mer	seafood
des moules	mussels
des crudités	raw vegetables

Au restaurant

j'ai faim	I'm hungry
un repas	meal
l'addition	bill
le plat du jour	dish of the day
les plats régionaux	local dishes
service compris	service included
un pourboire	tip
le serveur	waiter
Garçon!	waiter!
saignant	rare
à point	medium
bien cuit	well done
Bon appétit!	enjoy your meal!

Body (le corps)

le bras   arm
*(think: flex your biceps to show you are **bra**ve)*
la jambe   leg
*(think: messy breakfast-eater drops **jam** on leg)*
la tête   head
(think: the accent is like a little hat on a head)

les oreilles	ears
*(think: hear people shout "**ooray!**")*	
les épaules	shoulders
(think: "*hey Paul!*" you slap his shoulder…)	
le nez	nose
(think: horse with long nose saying "**neigh**")	
les dents	teeth
*(think: **dent**ist)*	
le dos (pronounced "doh")	back
*(think: **back door** sounds like back – dos)*	
la main	hand
*(think: the **main thing** you need to do anything)*	
le pied	foot
*(think: « **pied**estrian »)*	
la bouche	mouth
les yeux (pronounced "yer"	eyes
le ventre / l'estomac	stomach
les genoux	knees

Health (la santé)

garder la forme	to keep fit
rester en bonne santé	to stay healthy
il faut / on doit	one must
manger sainement	to eat healthily
manger équilibré	eat a balanced diet
s'entrainer	to train
faire du sport	to do sport

éviter le sucre		to avoid sugar
la malbouffe		junk food
bien que ce soit bon		although it's tasty
bouger	t	to move around
je fais un regime		I'm on a diet
il ne faut pas		one should not
ca fait grossir		it makes you fat
fumer		to smoke
se droguer		to take drugs
boire de l'alcool		to drink alcohol
devenir accro		to get addicted
déprimé		depressed
prévenir		to prevent
de graves maladies		serious illnesses
l'obésité		obesity
le sida		AIDS
de plus en plus de		more and more
le cancer de poumons		lung cancer
les crises cardiaques		heart attacks
des comprimés		pills
tousser		to cough
j'ai mal à la tête / au bras		my head / arm hurts
je me suis cassé la jambe		I broke my leg
un rhume		a cold

| je suis enrhumé | I have a cold |
| la grippe | flu |

CLOTHES (Les vêtements)

Je porte	I wear
Je mets	I put on
On doit porter	we have to wear
un uniforme	uniform

> *Top tip:* Think about a man wearing the masculine clothes and a woman wearing the feminine clothes. It's a bit unfair, because just as with the house vocab, she gets a lot more than he does, even the shirt, tie, jacket, socks and shoes. He gets jeans, trousers, a Tshirt, a jumper, coat, hat and gloves.

un pull	jumper (pullover)
un t-shirt	Tshirt
un jean	jeans
un pantalon	trousers (pants long)
un manteau	coat (man, down to his toes)
un chapeau	hat (for a chap)
un imperméable	raincoat
des gants	gloves
une veste / un blouson	jacket (not vest!)
une casquette	cap (small helmet)
une écharpe	scarf
des chaussettes	socks (you need a set)
des chaussures	shoes (be sure of them)
bonnet	woolly hat

une robe	dress
une jupe	skirt
une chemise	shirt
une cravate	tie
une casque	helmet
des bottes	boots
en coton	cotton
en laine	wool
en soie	silk
en cuir	leather

Accessories (les accessoires)

des écouteurs	earphones *(from écouter)*
des bijoux	jewellery
des lunettes	glasses
du maquillage	make-up
un portable	mobile
un parapluie	umbrella

COLOURS (les couleurs)

rouge	red
orange	orange
jaune	yellow
vert(e)	green
bleu(e)	blue
rose	pink
violet	purple
blanc (blanche)	white

noir(e)	black
marron (*no plural*)	brown (chestnut)
gris(e)	grey

ANIMALS (les animaux)

un chien	a dog
un chat	a cat
un lapin	a rabbit
une vache	a cow
un cheval	a horse
un mouton	a sheep
un cochon	a pig
un cochon d'inde	a guinea pig
un serpent	a snake
un cheval (des chevaux)	a horse
un poisson	a fish

Sentences about pets

> **Top tip:** "s'appelle" means "is called", so use **qui** to say "**who** is called"
> If you don't have one it's je n'ai pas **DE**

J'ai un chien **qui** s'appelle	I have a dog called
Je n'ai pas **de** chien	I don't have a dog
Je n'ai pas **d'**animaux	I don't have a pet
Je voudrais **un** chien	I would like a dog
J'adore **les** chiens	I love dogs

TIME PHRASES

Il est neuf heures moins le quart	8.45
Il est deux heures et demie	2.30
Il est huit heures et quart	8.15
Il est trois heures vingt	3.20
Il est onze heures moins vingt	10.40
à minuit	at midnight
à midi	at midday
hier	yesterday
demain	tomorrow
dernier	last
prochain	next (ap**proaching**)
la semaine dernière	last week (note the e on both)
l'année dernière	last year (note the e on both)
le weekend dernier	last weekend (no e or accent)
le mois dernier	last month (no e or accent)
la semaine prochaine	next week (note the e on both)
l'année prochaine	next year (note the e on both)
le weekend prochain	next weekend
après avoir mangé	after eating
de temps en temps	sometimes
tous les jours	every day
le samedi	on Saturdays

DAYS OF THE WEEK

lundi	Monday
mardi	Tuesday
mercredi	Wednesday

jeudi	Thursday
vendredi	Friday *(get the van ready)*
samedi	Saturday
dimanche	Sunday
lundi	on Monday
le lundi	on Mondays
le weekend	at the weekend

MONTHS OF THE YEAR *(no capitals in French)*

janvier	January
février	February
mars	March
avril	April
mai	May
juin	June
juillet	July
aout	August
septembre	September
octobre	October
novembre	November
décembre	December

SEASONS

au printemps	in Spring *("oh! it's Spring!")*
en été	in Summer
en automne	in Autumn
en hiver	in Winter

à Pâques	at Easter
à Noël	at Christmas

Negative expressions

Je ne mange pas	I don't eat
Je ne mange jamais	I never eat
Je ne mange plus	I no longer eat
Je ne mange que	I only eat fruit
Je ne mange rien	I don't eat anything
Je ne vois personne	I don't see anyone
Personne ne le fait	Nobody does it

GRAVE ACCENT WORDS

There aren't many of these in words that are commonly used, but don't lose marks unnecessarily by forgetting the ones you should know.

après	after
très	very
près de	near
mère / père	mother, father
frère	brother
derrière	last
derrière	behind
à (eg à gauche / à Londres)	at / to (on the left)
où	where
là	there
Je me lève	I get up
J'espère	I hope

J'achète	I buy
Je préfère (sad eyebrow accents)	I prefer
problème	problem
déjà	already
élève	pupil
collège	school
bibliothèque	library
matière	subject
complètement	completely
mystère	mystery

Here's a story to help you remember the words :

Where do I live?   I live **there**, in a **very** big house **near** London **behind** the **library**, with my **mother, father, brother, grandmother** and **grandfather**. I hope that when I **get up, I buy** something - but the **problem** is that I have to go to **school** and be a **pupil already** studying a **subject** and I **prefer** it to be **completely** a **mystery**

Using that story, see how many grave accent words you can remember and write them below:

VERY FRENCH THINGS

un Parisien	person from Paris
le TGV	train grande vitesse (fast train)
le SNCF	French railway company
le VTT	mountain biking
les randonnées	hikes
la chasse	hunting
la boulangerie	baker's shop
la pâtisserie	cake shop
quinze jours	a fortnight
le lycée	sixth form college
un lycéen	a sixth former
un département	similar to a "county" of France
les escargots	snails
en seconde	in year 12
en terminale	in year 13
redoubler	to repeat a year at school
le brevet	GCSE equivalent
un stage en entreprise	a work placement
préparer le bac	do do A levels

Synonyms

There is more than one way of expressing most things, and your passive vocabulary needs to be on full alert for the listening and reading papers. Listed below are all the different ways of expressing particular ideas. Just take a look at the number of ways you can express *liking* for a start...

Liking

j'aime

j'adore

ça me plait

ça me fait plaisir

c'est bon

je l'aime

ça fait du bien

ça m'a plu

c'est agréable

intéressant

passionnant

ça me passionne

ça m'intéresse

c'est mon truc

j'y suis accro

Agreement

d'accord

tu as raison

Disliking

je déteste / j'ai horreur de

j'en ai marre

ça m'embête / ça m'énerve

ce n'est pas mon truc

Students

les élèves

les lycéens

les étudiants

Home

a domicile

a la maison

au foyer

A method, manner or way

une méthode

une façon / manière

un moyen

To talk

parler de

discuter

bavarder

Annoying

Enervant / embêtant

casse-pieds

Disagreement

tu as tort

tu n'as pas raison

tu dis des bêtises

Jobs

un travail

un poste

un emploi

un boulot

un métier

une carrière

Expressing opinions

je trouve

je pense / je crois

j'ai l'impression

à mon avis

selon moi

Cheap

bon marché

pas cher

moins cher

moins couteux

Not allowed

on ne peut pas

c'est interdit

impossible

pas permis

il ne faut pas

on n'a pas le droit

Essential

il faut / on doit

c'est essentiel / obligatoire

il n'y a pas de choix

Food

la nourriture

les aliments

l'alimentation

Always

toujours

sans exception

dans tous les cas

sans arrêter

To keep healthy

rester en / garder la forme

avoir une bonne santé

To move

Bouger

se déplacer

circuler

déménager

Funny

Drôle / marrant / rigolo

il me fait rire

Ça me fait sourire

Teacher

Un / une prof

Instituteur / institutrice

enseignant(e)

Angry

en colère, fâché

furieux

de mauvaise humeur

Shops

Les grandes surfaces

le centre commercial

les magasins

les commerces

les boutiques

Asking questions

The role play will require you, amongst other things, to formulate questions. When asking a question to which the answer is yes or no, just say the statement in a questioning voice:

Je dois payer?	Do I have to pay?
On doit sortir?	Do we have to go out?
On peut sortir?	Can we go out?
Tu veux venir?	Do you want to come?
Il va faire beau?	Will the weather be good?
Tu a bien dormi?	Did you sleep well?
C'est ouvert?	Is it open?
C'est fermé?	Is it closed?
C'est loin du camping?	Is it far from the campsite?
C'est près du camping?	Is it near the camp site?

Est-ce que.... Alternative

Alternatively, you can turn those statements into questions as above but insert est-ce que just before it:

Est-ce que c'est ouvert ?	Is it open?
Est-ce qu'on doit payer ?	Do we have to pay?
Est-ce que je peux venir ?	Can I come?
Est-ce qu'il va faire beau ?	Will the weather be good?
Est-ce que l'eau est chaude ?	Is the water hot?

Questions using question words

À quelle heure = *when (at what time)*

À quelle heure part le train ?	When does the train leave?
À quelle heure êtes-vous arrivé ?	When did you arrive?
À quelle heure sors-tu ?	What time do you go out?

Quand = *when (generally)*

Quand est ton anniversaire ?	When is your birthday?
Quand allons-nous manger ?	When are we going to eat?
Quand as-tu vu le film ?	When did you see the film?

Comment = *how / what's it like*

Comment vas-tu au collège ?	How do you go to school?
Comment a-t-il trouvé le film ?	How did he find the film?
Comment est ton frère ?	What's your brother like?

Où = *where*

Où est la gare ?	Where is the station?
Où est le magasin ?	Where is the shop?
Où as-tu mis mon sac ?	Where did you put my bag?

Combien de = *how many*

Combien de frères as-tu ?	How many brothers have you?
Pour combien de personnes ?	For how many people?
Pour combien de nuits ?	For how many nights?

Pourquoi = *why*

Pourquoi es-tu triste ?	Why are you sad?
Pourquoi a-t-il acheté le chat ?	Why did he buy the cat?
Pourquoi doit-on partir ?	Why do we have to leave?

Qui = *who*

Qui as-tu invitè ?	Who have you invited?
Qui allons-nous voir ?	Who are we going to see?
Qui aimes-tu ?	Who do you like?

Que OR Qu'est-ce que = *what*

Qu'est-ce que c'est ?	What is it?
Qu'est-ce que tu penses ?	What do you think?
Que penses-tu ?	What do you think?
Qu'est-ce que tu as fait ?	What have you done?
Qu'as-tu fait ?	What have you done?
Qu'est-ce que tu veux ?	What do you want?
Que veux-tu ?	What do you want?
Qu'est-ce qu'il y a ?	What is there?
Qu'y a-t-il ?	What is there?

Understanding instructions in the role play

Some exam boards require candidates to understand instructions in the role play such as:

Réagissez avec plaisir	React with pleasure
Posez une question	Ask a question
Répondez à la question	Answer the question
Expliquez la situation	Explain the situation
Saluez votre ami	Say hello to your friend
Dites ce que vous faites	Say what you're doing
Proposez de payer	Offer to pay
Expliquez pourquoi	Explain why
Demandez le prix	Ask the price
Faites vos excuses	apologise

False friends (faux amis)

La location DOESN'T MEAN LOCATION - it means **rental**
Location (place) is endroit, lieu

La librairie DOESN'T MEAN LIBRARY - it means **bookshop**
A library is a "bibliothèque"

Personne DOESN'T just MEAN person - It can mean **nobody**
To say a person it's "UNE personne"

Passer les examens DOESN'T MEAN PASS - it means **take**
To say pass you say "reussir" = succeed

Un roman DOESN'T MEAN ROMAN - it means **novel**
Roman in French is "romain"

La journée DOESN'T MEAN JOURNEY - it means **day**
A journey in French is "un voyage"

Travailler DOESN'T MEAN TRAVEL - it means **to work**
Travel in French is "voyager"

Assister DOESN'T MEAN ASSIST - it means **to attend**
Assist in French is "aider"

Raisins DOESN'T MEAN RAISINS - it means **grapes**
Raisins are "raisins secs"

THE WORDS EVERYONE FORGETS

sans	without
presque	almost *(nearly)*
devant	in front of
souvent	often *(Sue visits often)*
avant	before *(in advance)*
derrière	behind
loin	far *(lions are far away)*
pour	to (with infinitive) or for
quel / quelle	which
qui	who
quand	when
combien de	how many
trop de	too many (with noun)
trop	too (with adj)
assez	quite (with adj)
surtout	especially, above all
déjà	already
heureusement	fortunately
malheureusement	unfortunately
toujours	always
tous les jours	every day
sauf	except
même	even
plus	more
ne ..... plus	no longer
jamais	never

NUMBERS

un	1
deux	2
trois	3
quatre	4
cinq	5
six	6
sept	7
huit	8
neuf	9
dix	10
onze	11
douze	12
treize	13
quatorze	14
quinze	15
seize	16
dix-sept	17
dix-huit	18
dix-neuf	19
vingt	20
vingt-et-un etc	21
trente	30
quarante	40
cinquante	50
soixante	60
soixante-dix	70

J'ai treize ans
I am 13 *(I have 13 years)*

Il a douze ans
He is 12 *(he has 12 years)*

quatre-vingt	80
quatre-vingt-dix	90
cent	100

COUNTRIES AND CONTINENTS

Top Tip: Feminine countries and continents take "en" whether you are going TO the country or you are IN it.

Masculine countries take ""au"
Je vais au Portugal – I go to Portugal
Je suis en Portugal – I am in Portugal

Plural countries take "aux"
Je vais aux Etats-Unis – I go to the USA
Je suis aux Etats-Unis

Feminine – take "en"

La France	France
L'Angleterre	England
La Grande Bretagne	Great Britain
L'Ecosse	Scotland
L'Irlande	Ireland
L'Allemagne	Germany
L'Italie	Italy
La Belgique	Belgium
La Grèce	Greece
La Suède	Sweden
L'Europe	Europe
L'Amerique	America

| L'Australie | Australia |
| L'Asie | Asia |

Masculine – take "au"

Le Royaume Uni	UK
Le pays de Galles	Wales
Le Portugal	Portugal
Le Japon	Japan
Le Canada	Canada

Plural – take "aux"

| Les Etats Unis | USA |

NATIONALITIES *(NOTE NO INITIAL CAPITALS)*

anglais(e)	English
français(e)	French
espagnol(e)	Spanish
italien / italienne	Italian
portugais(e)	Portuguese
irlandais(e)	Irish
gallois(e)	Welsh
grec (grecque)	Greek
hollandais(e)	Dutch
suédois(e)	Swedish
japonais(e)	Japanese
autrichien / autrichienne	Austrian
canadien / canadienne	Canadian

belge	Belgian
australien / australienne	Australian
européen(ne)	European
américain(e)	American

Thank you for purchasing this book. I hope it has been helpful. If so, I would be very grateful if you would give the book a review on Amazon.

Please do look me up on YouTube as well where you will find some useful videos to prepare you for GCSE. I also have a Facebook page where I post special offers and freebies from time to time.

If you have any questions please do contact me through my website www.lucymartintuition.co.uk

You may also be interested in my other books, also available on Amazon:

How to Ace your French Oral

How to Ace your Spanish Oral

How to Ace your German Oral

Spanish vocabulary for GCSE

Common Entrance French Handbook

Brush up your French

Ten magic Tricks with French

Spanish in a Week

The French GCSE Handbook

The Spanish GCSE Handbook

Printed in Great Britain
by Amazon